Serial Killers

True Crime

10 In Depth True Stories Of Some Of The Most Savage Serial Killers And Criminals In History

Volume 4

Serial Killers True Crime

© **Copyright 2015 by Brody Clayton - All rights reserved.**

This document is geared towards providing exact and reliable information in regards to the topic and issue covered. The publication is sold with the idea that the publisher is not required to render accounting, officially permitted, or otherwise, qualified services. If advice is necessary, legal or professional, a practiced individual in the profession should be ordered.

- From a Declaration of Principles which was accepted and approved equally by a Committee of the American Bar Association and a Committee of Publishers and Associations.

In no way is it legal to reproduce, duplicate, or transmit any part of this document in either electronic means or in printed format. Recording of this publication is strictly prohibited and any storage of this document is not allowed unless with written permission from the publisher. All rights reserved.

The information provided herein is stated to be truthful and consistent, in that any liability, in terms of inattention or otherwise, by any usage or abuse of any policies, processes, or directions contained within is the solitary and utter responsibility of the recipient reader. Under no circumstances will any legal responsibility or blame be held against the publisher for any reparation, damages, or monetary loss due to the information herein, either directly or indirectly.

Respective authors own all copyrights not held by the publisher.

The information herein is offered for informational purposes solely, and is universal as so. The presentation of the information is without contract or any type of guarantee assurance.

The trademarks that are used are without any consent, and the publication of the trademark is without permission or backing by the trademark owner. All trademarks and brands within this book are for clarifying purposes only and are the owned by the owners themselves, not affiliated with this document.

Cover image courtesy of
https://www.flickr.com/photos/kessiye/170894085/

Serial Killers True Crime

Table of Contents

Introduction	vi
Chapter 1 : Cyanide Proposals	1
Chapter 2: Randy's Vices: Politics and Murder	10
Chapter 3: Hunting Feminine Prey	20
Chapter 4: Deadly Doodles	28
Chapter 5: The Singing Serial Killer	36
Chapter 6: Victim For Sale	44
Chapter 7: Impressing My Girlfriend, Svetlana	52
Chapter 8: Killing in Retirement Years	60
Chapter 9: Railway Station of Death	66
Chapter 10: Unstoppable Randall	78
Conclusion	84
Check Out My Other Books	85

Serial Killers True Crime
Like FREE books?

Would you like them delivered to you every week?

Do you like non-fiction books on a huge range of different topics?

We send out FREE e-books every week so we can share our books with the world!

We have FREE books every week on AMAZON that we send to our email list.

So if you want in, then visit the link at the end of this book to sign up and sit back and wait for new books to be sent straight to your inbox!

Introduction

I want to thank you for purchasing the book, *"Serial Killers True Crimes: 10 In Depth True Stories Of Some Of The Most Savage Serial Killers And Criminals In History"*.

If someone informed you that there was a serial killer roaming the area, what would you do? The normal response is to be more cautious: lock the doors, don't open them to strangers and always carry something for self-defense such as pepper spray.

If each of us did this, do you think the number of victims would still pile up? Maybe, maybe not. Read the following cases and discover how one person (or in the Copeland's case, two) became capable of slaying multiple victims despite people's knowledge of a serial killer's presence.

Thanks again, I hope you enjoy this book!

Serial Killers True Crime

Chapter 1 : Cyanide Proposals

Anitha Moolya was supposed to be getting married. She prepared for the big day by making an effort to look her best; she fixed her hair, dressed herself in an off-white sari, accentuated it with fresh flowers, and glass bangles. To complete the look, she wore a pair of gold earrings and a new pair of shoes.

It was to be perfect. Only, she didn't know that it was a farce from the very beginning.

The ceremony was to be held in a temple, so Anitha and her boyfriend went to the bus station in Hassan. Anticipating the travel, she decided to go to the women's rest room as her husband-to-be waited nearby.

The man, Anand Kulal, never expected her to return; in fact, when he saw that a lot of people had gathered in front of the toilet, he knew that he had accomplished his goal. The woman to whom he had promised marriage, was now dead.

As quiet as the wind, he started to walk away from the station until he disappeared into the nameless crowds. Soon enough, he reached the hotel where he and Anitha had stayed the night - he gathered their belongings and went quietly away.

The Misconception

Unknown to those who witnessed Anitha's collapse and death, she had been missing for quite some time now. Her family and friends, firmly believed that she had been victimized by the "Love Jihad" - a phenomenon in which Muslim men were encouraging Hindu women into Islamic conversion.

While Anitha's loved ones kept on protesting against it, the real perpetrator was at large. He was roaming the area, appearing as a gentleman, seducing women into marriage, and then afterwards, killing them by offering cyanide pills in the pretense that it was contraceptive medications.

Anand Kulal wasn't his real name, he was really Mohan Kumar, a former primary school teacher who killed women so he could get there valuables, like money and jewelry, and while he could camouflage his way into killing these women, the police would soon pick up his trail.

Anitha wasn't the only one...

What made the police suspicious about the crime was the frequency of its occurrence - 4 women suffered the same fates after Anitha and in 2009, nine more women were killed. The victims were all from different areas, like Hassan, Mysore, Bangalore, and Madikere.

The modus operandi was simple: Mohan Kumar would hunt for working women that came from middle-class or lower class families. He would then seduce them, until a marriage proposal was in order.

Mohan wouldn't ask for a dowry - he simply requested the wedding be kept secret and that they would start anew in another place. It explained why the families of the victims didn't know what happened to their loved ones, why they suddenly went away without telling anyone.

After the woman agreed to the marriage, they would check into a hotel, have sex on the night before the wedding, and then he'd give her cyanide in the pretense that it was a contraceptive pill. The Police even indicated that the reason why women trusted Mohan was because of his strategy to disguise himself as a man who had the same social status as his victim (caste). He did this by changing his name, thus, when the investigation concluded, the law authorities found out that he had used 12 aliases.

Officers also added that the most appealing part of the marriage proposal was the lack of dowry; not only did it mean less expenses, it would also make the woman believe that the man truly loved her. That didn't mean though, that the victim wouldn't own anything of value.

For one, the fact that she was working meant she had money of her own, she could withdraw it from the bank and give it to Mohan, or he could steal it from them. Secondly, since she was expecting marriage, she would bring her best clothes and most expensive jewelry with her - things which Mohan Kumar was after. One of Mohan's victims, Sunanda Poojari, even took 25,000 Rs from the bank before her marriage.

Tracking Mohan Cyanide

Like most serial killers, Mohan was caught because he wasn't careful enough - for instance, his cellphone number. Once the news of Anitha's demise reached her family, they became dedicated to finding justice for their daughter. They wanted to know what made her leave their home in secrecy and who was responsible for her death.

Her mobile phone was recovered from her belongings on the day she died and it contained Mohan's contact number. Anitha's family knew no one with the name Anand Kulal, so they deemed it important to investigate him. Fortunately, Mohan Kumar used just one mobile number to converse with all his victims; this knowledge became a vital piece of evidence.

From there, the police were able to track him down in his third wife, Sridevi Rai's house in Deralakatta Village near Mangalore. In their residence, the Police recovered numerous things which could link him to the other disappearances: visiting cards and fake identities using different names, gold ornaments (which appeared to belong to women), government seals and rubber stamps, and the most important - the cyanide bottles.

Like other serial killers, he also kept a record: there was a diary which contained the names of the women he approached. If a woman didn't accept his proposal, he crossed it out by marking it in red. Police stated that his success rate was 20%, small, to be honest, but since lives were at stake, any number is a big number.

Aside from the cellphone number, he also made a mistake when checking into hotels: while he used various names, his address stayed the same. His handwriting was also examined and it matched the check-in forms he filled out in the lodges he stayed in with each victim. Further investigation also revealed that Mohan deposited gold and jewelry using his own name - all of these were taken back and were used in court as evidence during his trial.

A Serial Killer's Development

Mohan Kumar was a primary school science teacher until he was kicked out of his job in 2005. The reason for his dismissal was attempted murder - apparently, his first attempt consisted of pushing a woman into a river. The woman was rescued and the case was submitted to a local court. After a court settlement, Mohan thought of a more effective way of killing.

Authorities believed that he learned of cyanide poisoning from a goldsmith who used it for polishing gold. He may have disguised himself as a goldsmith to be able to acquire cyanide from a chemist in Puttur. The rest as they say, is history. From 2005 to 2009, the year he was arrested, Mohan Kumar had killed at least 20 women.

Mohan in Jail

Mohan Kumar was known as Prisoner # 2395 in Mangalore District Jail. Unlike ordinary inmates, he was placed in a Quarantine Cell. Most of his time was spent reading, either law books or newspapers, as if he was gathering information to use to free himself. Mohan Kumar always appeared confident; he was 46 years old, but he looked younger, with a healthy mop of black hair and a thick mustache.

It appears that he used his charisma and good looks to seduce his victims. Police officers said he was intelligent - intelligence which made him even more vicious. After the initial court proceedings, Mohan talked to all the people concerned in the cases - which consisted of three murders.

He told them that he couldn't afford a great lawyer, but he was afraid that the government-appointed attorney wouldn't fight for his defense effectively. He even had the audacity to accuse the government of "tutoring" the witnesses, which at that time reached between 60-75. All the things spread about him were also lies, Mohan insisted.

Despite the police's confidence, they admitted that their case wasn't as airtight as they liked to believe. Mohan Kumar and his team were more than willing to point out their weaknesses: for instance, in the three cases they had, only one was killed via cyanide poisoning. Second, there were no "direct" witnesses - all of them were members of the victims' family or friends.

The Police Refused to Give Up

The prosecution may not be as solid as they needed it to be, but they collected all the evidence they could obtain. In fact, a breakthrough came when a priest, Eshwar Bhat, told the police that a day after Anitha's murder, Mohan approached him, asking how he could "wash away" the sin of killing someone.

The priest was shocked - he didn't know why it was the topic of their conversation, but he didn't pry. It was his job to answer him, so he told him to offer *Kumkuma archana* (which is a ritualistic offering to a god or deity), which Mohan did.

After a thorough investigation and deliberation, the judges decided that Mohan was guilty - and since he had taken at least 20 lives, he should also be given the same punishment: on December 2013, after a long fight from both the defense and the prosecution, Mohan Kumar was sentenced to death.

Chapter 2: Randy's Vices: Politics and Murder

On March 19, 1945, Randy Steven Kraft was born in Long Beach, California. Originally, his family was from Wyoming, but when the First World War started, they decided to move. His father, Harold, worked as a production worker, while Randy's mother, Opal, was a machine operator; Randy was the fourth child and was the only son in the family.

They never lived extravagantly, but Harold always made sure that there was a roof over their heads and food in their stomachs; even Opal, who took various jobs to add to her husband's wages, always found the time to guide the children.

The same can't be said for Harold, though, because while he was a good provider, emotionally, he was detached. In other words, while growing up, Randy was taken cared of by his three older sisters and a dedicated mother.

In 1948, when Randy was just three years old, the family moved again, this time to Midway City, California near Orange County. This was where Randy grew up to be an intelligent young man, as he flourished in his mother's and sisters' care. In 1957, many teachers believed that Randy was prepared to enter accelerated classes for 17th Street Junior High School.

A Good Fate Turning Sour

His intelligence took him to Westminster High School, where he, along with two other friends, established the Westminster World Affairs Club. Young Randy's dreams, according to reports, was to be a US Senator - not surprising, especially when he took a stand for his political views and wanted to become a Republican.

This goal was further sealed when he went into college (Claremont Men's College) and took a Bachelor of Arts in Economics. Teachers and schoolmates knew him to be smart and polite; he dated a few girls, but despite that, many still suspected that he was gay. In Claremont, he joined the Reserve Officer Training Corp.

His political inclination also grew, in fact, in 1964, he became an avid supporter and active campaigner of Barry Goldwater, a presidential candidate. In 1965, he worked as a bartender in a gay bar, and in those times, acquaintances noted his increasing need for Valium to remedy his headaches and stomach pains.

Despite these aches, he was still able to obtain his Economics degree in 1968, but at this point, his political views shifted - he started supporting Robert Kennedy, a known Democrat. Shortly after graduation, he chose to enlist in the US Air Force. His application was immediately accepted because he scored high in his aptitude tests, he had a good background, and had no "dirty" secrets.

Randy was assigned to Edwards Air Force Base. Whilst at the Edwards Base, he spoke with his family and told them about his homosexuality - his father was outraged, but his mother was more understanding, although it was obvious that she disapproved of his preference. After some time, the family came to accept his orientation and he remained in contact with them.

His sisters however, noticed that he was distancing himself from the family who loved and accepted him. A year later, Randy was dismissed from his USAF duties due to "medical" reasons (but it happened right after he disclosed to his superior that he was gay). Randy tried to challenge this decision, even going so far as to hiring a lawyer, but his superiors wouldn't budge, so he returned to his bar-tending job.

In 1971, the decomposing remains of Wayne Joseph Dukette were recovered near Ortega Highway. Wayne was a 30 year old bartender, a gay man, whom authorities believed to have been Randy's first kill, although there was no sign of foul play.

Then on March 29, 1975, Keith Daven Crothwell hitched a ride with Randy Kraft. One month later, the severed head of the 19 year old high school dropout was discovered. Police combed the freeway for the vehicle which Keith was last seen getting into and the search led them to Randy Steven Kraft.

Kraft insisted that after driving around for a while he had left Keith alive and well on the side of the road. Since there was no body (only a severed head) and the cause of death couldn't be ascertained, the court was not able to charge Randy with murder, hence, his killing spree continued for 8 more years.

The Birth of the (Freeway) Killer

In the article written by J.J. Maloney, he courageously

said that Randy Steven Kraft wasn't the Freeway Killer - that it was in fact, William Bonin, who was executed in San Quentin, California in 1966. He even insisted that if the police called Randy The Freeway Killer, they too were wrong.

It all began in 1972, when the police started discovering dead bodies of young men (often the victims were Marines) along the trails of Southern California - particularly from Long Beach, to Orange County, and to San Diego.

The cases had varying "signatures": some victims had burnt left nipples (the weapon used could have been a vehicle cigarette lighter), other victims suffered from mutilated left testicles (the dismemberment was done while the victim was still alive), and in some of cases, a foreign object was inserted into their anus.

The most solid link, however, could be found inside - all of them had ingested alcohol mixed with drugs (the most common was Valium). Due to these varied signatures (sometimes the victim wasn't tortured at all), the police had difficulty assessing if there was only one killer, or if there were more. They leaned more towards believing there was only one.

In Dennis McDougal's 1991 book entitled *Angel of Darkness*, he labeled Randy's killings as "the most heinous murder spree in history". While J.J. Maloney said he was wrong, no one could blame Dennis from voicing this opinion, after all, the crimes were truly heinous. One victim even had his eyelids cut, just so he wouldn't be able to close his eyes while the torture was happening.

Between 1972 to 1975, these tortures and killings kept on happening. In 1976, there was only one murder and the same in 1977, and because the police didn't disclose these two murders to the media, the public believed that the killings had stopped in 1975.

Bouncing Back

Everyone was surprised when in 1978, 14 people were killed in the span of 1 year and 8 months - from April 16, 1978 to December 13, 1979. This time, the police became even more cautious - they didn't give out any information aside from the victims' names, serial number, and their rank.

It was in January of 1980 when J.J. Maloney was asked to

be an investigative reporter for the *Register*; his goal was to collect as much data as he could about the cases because even if the police didn't directly agree on the presence of a serial killer, it was becoming obvious that there was one.

There were two problems during that time: first the lack of the information from the police made it hard for some people to consider having two murderers working at the same time. Second, the cases were not that well publicized.

While J.J. Maloney couldn't do anything about the first, he was able to remedy the second problem with the help of Dr. Albert Rosenstein, a forensic psychologist who said that the serial killer must be named - to make him more solid in the eyes of the people, hence the term, Freeway Killer.

It worked, because after the article "*'Freeway Killer' Cruises For Murder*" was released in March 24, 1980, the public started to accept that a serial killer was on the loose. Only, The Freeway Killer wasn't Randy Steven Kraft - this was proven when William Bonin was captured in June 11, 1980 and it was discovered that he had killed between August 1979 to June 1980 (the murders being referred to as the Freeway Killings), his victims comprised 21 young men. After his arrest, the killings continued and the police were at their wits' end.

Arresting the Southern California Strangler

After the Freeway Killer was arrested, the differences in the killing methods became apparent. When William Bonin was placed in custody, all the victims that followed were tortured. Apparently, while William Bonin killed young men, he had no penchant for torturing and mutilating them, unlike Randy Kraft.

On top of that Bonin would dispose of his victims by stopping his vehicle and dumping them on the freeway whereas Randy would throw them out of a fast-moving vehicle, most of the time causing severe damage to the already lifeless body.

It was clear that there were two (later on it would be three) killers, and only one was in custody - so the search continued and only ended three years later, on March 14, 1983. On that day, Highway Patrol officer Michael Sterling saw a vehicle driving erratically on the San Diego

Freeway.

Suspecting that the driver was under the influence of either drugs or alcohol, he set out to stop the car. The driver pulled over and got out - a few minutes and some sobriety tests later, he was proven to be drunk. Another officer, Sgt. Michael Howard, inspected the car and in the passenger seat he found the strangled body of 25 year old Terry Gambrel, a US Marine and Randy Kraft's last victim.

From here, everything went smoothly: the car contained other evidence, such as alcohol, tranquilizers, and blood, which didn't belong to Terry Gambrel (suggesting there were other victims). In Randy's house were creepy photos of the victims showing them either dead or simply unconscious.

Personal items of young men who had turned up missing in the last decade were also recovered. There was also a "coded diary" where Randy kept records of those he had killed (there were 61 entries but because four of which were double murders, there were at least 65 victims). One of the entries was also "unreadable" but police suspected it was Erich Church.

Terry Gambrel was his 67th victim. The list became known as the scorecard, that's why Randy Kraft was also known as the Scorecard Killer. He maintained his innocence even after he was found guilty of 16 homicides and was sentenced to death in November of 1989. As of now, Randy is still in San Quentin State Prison on death row and he still denies any connection to the murders.

Analysis

Why he did the things he did could be anyone's guess now; he appeared to have a good childhood, well-taken cared of and provided for. From various accounts, he was intelligent - he could have gotten a job easily and stayed in it as long as he liked. At the time of his arrest, he was in a relationship with a live-in partner.

Could it be his lack of a relationship with his father? Or the initial disapproval of his family over his sexuality? Perhaps it was the rejection from the military? Who knows? One can only assume.

Chapter 3: Hunting Feminine Prey

Robert Hansen was a hunter and he found Alaska to be *the* perfect place for the chase. The terrain, the lighting (or the lack thereof), and the wilderness made all his prey cower in fear - there was no one to hear their screams, no one to give a helping hand. All these, for Robert, made the hunt even more exciting.

Alaska: 1971 – 1983

From 1971 to 1983, a game was played in Alaska, mostly in Anchorage. The game master was Robert Hansen - he created the rules, which weren't many, and ended the game when the targets were subdued. For 12 years, he would roam the area, seeking his next prey, which, after his capture, amounted to 17 women, although only 12 bodies were ever recovered.

Other intelligence agencies suggested that the number of victims could reach up to 37, but proving it would be a little hard now. Aside from the murders, the hunter and game master also admitted to raping 30 women, but not once did he show any sign of regret, sympathy, or remorse.

If law authorities could be asked why this case got the spotlight, the answer would probably be instantaneous: firstly, it was the only killing spree in Alaska where the victims, women, were kidnapped and then thrust toward the Alaskan wilderness only to be hunted down and killed.

Secondly was the fact that in 1983, no other evidence was used to gain a search warrant for Hansen's properties other than a psychological profile.

Robert Hansen

Robert Christian Hansen was originally from Estherville, Iowa. He was born on February 15, 1939 to his baker father (who was a Danish immigrant) and his wife. Growing up wasn't a breeze for young Bob, because his father was strict, often times forcing him to work long hours in the bakery.

Robert's confidence level were low, partly because of his acne condition and partly because of his stutter, which according to some reports, was made worse by stress from home, work, and school.

On top of that, he was forced to use his right hand even though he was left handed - this too, resulted in stress. In other words, young Robert was a loner, someone with few social skills. The first clue that he could be a serial killer in the making emerged on December 7, 1960, when 21 year old Robert asked a 16 year old employee in their bakery to help him burn a school bus garage (this was for revenge, against the abuse he thought the Pocahontas, Iowa people were suffering).

Fortunately, the teenager had some morals, so he turned himself and Robert in to the police. Robert was sentenced to spend three years in prison, and upon learning this, his wife (of only 6 months) divorced him. Instead of spending 3 years, he only spent 20 months after parole was granted - which was surprising, considering his diagnosis of Infantile Personality Disorder (a sub type of attention-seeking Histrionic disorder) which made him more inclined to seek revenge.

A few months after he was released, Robert found a new wife, and occasionally, he would steal - not because he needed the money (or the valuables), he just enjoyed the thrill of it. As unbelievable as it sounds, no charges were ever laid in relation to those thefts. In 1967, Robert thought it was time to start anew - he decided to head to Alaska.

Paradise

Once in Anchorage, Alaska, Robert discovered his desire to hunt - the wilderness was perfect for the thrill he was looking for, so he took advantage of it. Only 2 years after moving, in 1969 (as well as in 1970 and 1971), he was already able to enter 4 animals in the Pope-Young Club Records.

Pope-Young Club was North America's leading bow hunting and conservation organization. On their website, they even encourage those who like a fair chase, those who are ethical bow hunters, and those who care to preserve the culture, to join the club.

In 1971, however, Robert knew that hunting animals was already a piece of cake - he needed more adventure. The timing of his search was just right; during that time, Anchorage was plagued with pornography and prostitution - women were lured into "dancing" jobs under the pretense of a good wage, and many females found it appealing.

On top of this, there were also robberies, riots, street beatings, firebombs, and other murders and as a result the police were busy, too busy to notice Robert and his hunting escapades. For Robert Hansen, it was a paradise; all he had to do was show a woman $300 and she would go with him anywhere he directed her to.

He didn't appear dangerous, as one rape victim pointed out; he looked like the perfect dork, especially with his glasses on. But once inside the car, the psychopath in him would be released. His rape cases never yielded any punishment, since at times, he wasn't even identified as the perpetrator (or a complaint wasn't made).

On the occasions that a victim positively identified him, law authorities would believe his version over that of the prostitute - after all, even his neighbors attested that he was a good man. The murders, albeit a little wild in concept, were actually well calculated. In the vastness of Alaska, there would be no witnesses, and if there was, Robert would take care of it.

He even killed a dog in the fear that it would lead the police to the shallow grave he had dug for his victim. In 1977, Robert stole a chainsaw and was sentenced to 5 years in prison; however, he only served one.

Psychiatric reports insisted that he was a danger to society - but the court only ordered him to undergo lithium therapy to manage his mood swings. This order was never enforced inside the prison, or after he was released.

If only his entire 5 year sentence had been served, some lives could have been saved from The Hunter. As soon as he was a free man, Robert Hansen killed again.

"Robert is a good man."

As the body count rose, Robert Hansen worked double time to develop a good reputation using illegal methods. He staged a fake burglary at his home, claiming that the wildlife trophies he had were stolen, when the truth was, he had hidden them in his backyard. The insurance money amounted to $13,000 and he used it to build a bakery.

When the staged burglary was discovered, he stated that the trophies turned up in his backyard and he had just forgotten to call his insurance agent. Of course no one ever heard of this fraud; they just saw Robert as how he wanted to be seen - a good man.

Arrest and Conviction

The next year, he purchased a small plane even though he didn't have a pilot's license. The plane, a Piper Super Cub, would become one of his primary tools in his hunts. Reports said that he would fly his victims from Fourth Avenue to Knick River (often at knife or gun-point), before raping, torturing, and murdering them.

The charter map he had was filled with marks of the locations where he buried his prey - the most common being the Knick River. When one of the rape victims decided to testify against him, the police decided to use it as a springboard to connect him to the unsolved cases of missing women.

Although the Anchorage Police Department only had a criminal profile and no solid proof, they were still granted a search warrant to comb Robert's property, where they found numerous pieces of evidence to pin him down. His downfall was his own doing because Robert was a known trophy collector; while his den was filled with legitimate trophies, his basement was stuffed with illegal ones.

One of the items found was a fish necklace belonging to Andrea Altiery (one of the victims.) No one could mistake it for someone else's because the necklace was custom made for Andrea. The search warrant was immediately followed by an arrest warrant on the same day (October 27, 1983).

A few months down the line, with various evidence gathered, as well as Robert's help with locating the bodies (only 12 were found), he was sentenced to serve 461 years in prison without parole eligibility on February 27, 1984.

The Pope-Young Club issued a statement saying that while Robert's crimes (which consisted of rape, murder, fraud, theft, and assault) would not invalidate his bow hunting records, they still removed his name from their registry.

Robert's wife and his two children attempted to keep their lives in tact, but after two years of harassment and bullying (especially to the children), the wife filed for a divorce and they moved away.

Chapter 4: Deadly Doodles

From January of 1974 to September of 1975, one man caught the interest of the patrons of Castro's Bar (and other gay bars) - the man, who was an African-American according to many witnesses, would often "doodle" a cartoon caricature of a patron and give it to them as a simple gift.

May be it was the talent, or the sheer simplicity of the act that made some patrons want to get to know him better, so in the end, he or she would leave the bar together with the Black Doodler and head out to somewhere more private where they would become more acquainted. No one from the bar would suspect that the Doodler was a killer.

The First Victim

Police reports said the Doodler's first victim was previous John Doe #7; he was found on January 27, 1974, at around 1:57 am near San Francisco's Ocean Beach, supine, and bearing multiple stab wounds. The large wounds on his hands and arm depicted a struggle and attempt to defend himself.

He was well-clothed and valuables such as his Timex watch and cash of $21.12 were still with him. Later on, he would be identified as Gerald Earl Cavanaugh, aged 49.

The number of victims after Gerald couldn't be extracted as the Doodler was never caught. Some reports said he was responsible for up to 14 killings, while others said only 5 or 6. The only sure thing about the case was it wasn't given as much attention as the other unsolved serial killings such as the Zodiac Killer.

Experts said it was because of the timing; a year before the killing started, the American Psychiatric Association Board of Trustees stopped identifying homosexuality as a disorder, and a few years after the killings, San Francisco's Ken Horne was diagnosed with Kaposi's Sarcoma. The Doodler Killings didn't rate a coverage, hence, it was quickly forgotten.

The Impersonator and the German National

Almost 5 months after Gerald Earl Cavanaugh's body was discovered, a second victim, a homosexual impersonator, followed. A woman (who was never identified) saw his body at Spreckel's Lake at the Golden Gate Park on June 25, 1974. The Victim was Joseph "Jae" Stevens; he had been stabbed three times, his nose and mouth were bloodied, and the police theorized that he had even driven his killer to the murder site.

Jae Stevens was born in Texas and had been an employee at Finocchio's, a club which had been established since the 1930s. At first the bar was opened for gay men, but when the 70s came and discrimination took its toll on the business, homosexuals looked elsewhere to have fun. Jae first worked there (8 years ago) as an impersonator of famous female celebrities, but through the years, he shifted to gay comedy.

More than a week after Jae's murder, Claus A. Christmann, 31, was found dead; he was last seen alive in Bojangles. Claus was a Michelin employee and the Doodler's third victim.

On July 7, 1974, a woman named Tauba Weiss was innocently walking her dog when the dog, Moondance, suddenly barked and ran towards where a man was lying, unmoving. Tauba instantly knew he was dead, so she called the police, who responded immediately.

After the initial investigation, they found the man to be Claus A. Christmann, a German National. By the time he was discovered, Claus was wearing a tan leather jacket and a wedding ring; there was also a tube of makeup in his pocket, suggesting that even though he was married, he could still be gay.

David Toschi, an inspector who arrived at the scene, called it one of the most vicious stabbings he'd ever seen - and since he also investigated the Zodiac Killings, people believed him. When Claus' murder was investigated, the police began to suspect that the three murders were connected.

According to them, the similarities were as follows: all the victims were stabbed in both the front and back, they all seemed to have met someone who suggested a drive to a remote area such as the Ocean Beach and Golden Gates Park, and all of them were stripped of any identification.

Since Claus was a German National, who had a wife and two kids in Germany, the police were forced to send the body to them even though his killer still hadn't been identified. He appeared to have been in the area for almost three months before the murder took place.

Perhaps one of the problems that made the Doodler Killings so underrated was the amount of effort (or the lack thereof) the police poured into solving the case; the 1970s was a transition where a gay person could be courageous enough to "come out", but most of the population was not keen on accepting them.

If, for example, a gay man was beaten, or robbed, the police would only think that they had it coming. Sure they would do their job, but not to the extent of being dedicated. When the Doodler killings happened, the reaction was almost the same - it was as if the victim was at fault.

The Fourth

Almost a year after Claus A. Christmann was slain, another corpse was recovered courtesy of the Doodler. On May 12, 1975, a hiker found the body of Frederick Elmer Capin, aged 32, in the dunes between Ulloa and Vicente Street. Frederick was six foot tall and 148 pounds; his t-shirt was soaked in his own blood from the stab wounds he had endured from his assailant.

Autopsy reports indicated that the cause of death was a deep stab wound to his heart, particularly to his aorta. Inspecting the sand dunes, the authorities concluded that since there were marks, Frederick must have been dragged by the killer for about 20 feet before he decided to abandon him.

Unlike other victims, there was no indication that Frederick was gay; in fact, his profession seemed very masculine. Reports said that he was a "medical corpsman" in the Navy and was even awarded with a "commendation medal" for saving 4 people in the Vietnam War.

The Last

Herald Gullberg was 66 years old; reports said he was suffering from cirrhosis of the liver. The unfortunate thing was, his murderer wasn't his liver, it was the Doodler. On June 4, 1975, a hiker found his corpse on a golf course in Lincoln Park. Unlike the other victims, Herald had been dead for almost two weeks before he was discovered, judging by the decomposition and the maggots present in his remains.

Like Frederick, there was no indication that Herald was gay, however, since the Doodler had the habit of picking his victims from gay bars, it was safe to assume that Herald visited at least one. Herald was a Swedish sailor and he spent a lot of time traveling to different countries, from China, Australia, and United States and in 1955, he became a naturalized citizen.

Finding the Doodler

Five months after Herald's body was discovered, the police released a composite sketch describing the Doodler, who "frequents bars and restaurants in Upper Market and Castro areas". The black killer was assumed to be only 19 to 22 years old, but he was lean and tall, probably 5'10" to six foot tall. Another known description was the navy-type watch cap he frequently wore.

His drawings were never released, but from reports coming from those who had a chance to brush elbows with him, he was a commercial art student. Police also believed that he was a quiet, serious, and educated man. As much as the authorities wanted to close the case, the lack of witnesses and the cleanliness of the crime scenes left them with little to no clues.

People were afraid to come forward to testify because they might reveal themselves as homosexuals. Still there were many "surviving" witnesses who approached the press to relate their stories on how they had escaped the Doodler. One was about a Los Angeles man who was about to sleep with a black man, however, when he noticed that a knife fell from the man's coat, he retreated.

Years and years later, and the Doodler was never captured. The crime rate for homosexuals increased, but it became impossible for the law authorities to identify which were the workings of the serial killer and which weren't. Herald may be the oldest and the last victim, but there could still be others.

Things could have been different if the media had paid more attention and the discrimination against homosexual men was not at its peak.

Chapter 5: The Singing Serial Killer

Verry Idham Henyansyah is a very interesting killer. When he was caught and placed in custody, he not only authored a book entitled: *Confessions: The Untold Story of Ryan* (because he also went by that name), but he also created a song album featuring 12 pop songs. Fittingly, he gave it the title, *My Last Performance* (it was released while he was on death row).

Ryan was an Indonesian serial killer who admitted to killing 11 people. In his autobiography, he related that he was a former Koran recital teacher and a model. True enough, while in prison, he was visited frequently by girls who wanted a photo with him.

Please Understand, Beloved

Many people believed him to be insane, for really, how could a man appear so casual when he was really a killer? Still, the Indonesian court believed that he was sane - that the murders were premeditated, and so, he was to be punished as any sane man should be.

One of his proven victims was Hery Santoso, whose body he dismembered into seven parts. Ryan placed the severed body parts in a plastic travel bag and a suitcase before dumping it along the roads of Jakarta in 2008.

The reason for the heinous crime was jealousy: apparently, Hery offered to pay Ryan with money and a car if he would let his (Ryan's) boyfriend sleep with him. To further prove this, one of the songs in Ryan's album was entitled, Please Understand, Beloved.

There Were Others

Everything wouldn't be as sensational as it was if Hery Santoso was the only victim, however, there were more, and Ryan had no qualms in admitting to them. During the investigation, he confessed to killing 11 people, and when they checked Ryan's parents' backyard, they found the remains of a mother and her three year old child (along with others).

Once the trial started, Ryan began his "habit" of entertaining the people in the court by singing the songs from his album. Despite this, the prosecution was not amused; they demanded death sentence for the unforgivable crimes he committed. According to them, Ryan wasn't insane when he committed the murders, neither was he hallucinating.

If anything, he was calculating; he planned the murder (Hery's), and the fact that he dismembered the body and kept the parts in suitcases meant that he planned to cover his tracks. Ryan, according to the prosecution, may have been scared of getting caught, but if he wasn't captured, he'd commit the crimes again.

When the judge declared the sentence, which was death, Ryan stood calmly and said that every one would die, and that he was ready for his death. Still, his family, especially his father, refused to give up because they believed that Ryan was insane - he shouldn't be punished, according to them. Appeals were applied for, but as of now, the death sentence still stands.

Confessions: The Untold Story of Ryan

31 year old Ryan thought that he had a lot to share, hence, when he was imprisoned, he busied himself with a masterpiece - an autobiography which depicted his life. In the book, one gets a glimpse of the childhood life of the

singing serial killer. According to him, he was a good boy, he always got good grades and would be included in the top of the class in both elementary and high school years.

When the time was right, he chose to become a Koran teacher, and ironically, he dated his first Koran instructor - the relationship started when he was 20 years old and it lasted for 9 years. After his career as a Koran teacher, he decided to become athletic. Ryan took a job as an aerobics instructor, and from time to time, he worked as a model.

His book, *Confessions*, went to print, and the initial run was 4,000 copies. The proceeds would be given to his mother. What bothered the authorities the most about his book was the sordid details he had included: for instance, there was a map to Ryan's parent's backyard in East Java which he hand-drew. In between a chicken coop, a septic tank, and a fishing tank, Ryan marked his victims' graves with the initials of their names. There were a total of 10 graves.

Ryan further explained that some of the murders were not premeditated, they were products of rage. An example was the murder of "Zaky" and "Askony". The two allegedly hurt Ryan with harsh words and they groped his privates to force him to date them. Ryan mentioned: "I hated their acts, especially when my homosexuality was used to satiate their lust."

As for the other victims (three men and one woman), Ryan said they infuriated him because they went to his house thinking that he would have sex with them. After fighting them physically and verbally, the four victims were killed. Ryan insisted in the book that he couldn't remember the other details of the killings.

In fact, he added: "If you ask me how I had the heart to kill the five victims, I cannot answer you with certainty because I don't recall all of it clearly."

The second last chapter of the book was dedicated to Hery Santoso's murder, which appeared to have taken place in Ryan's Depok, West Java Province apartment. Ryan detailed that when he woke up, he saw red, and only then did he realize that it was blood, and the meat all around him was human flesh.

In his interviews, Ryan added that once he saw the mess, he wanted nothing more than to get rid of him. The mother (whose body was also recovered in his parent's backyard) was also killed because of immense disgust. She had apparently seduced Ryan into having sex with her, so he killed her.

Afterwards, since the three year old child was a witness, he also got rid of her. This only goes to show that at some point, Ryan was coherent when he committed the crimes.

Analysis

Many experts believed that the reason why Ryan killed people had something to do with his homosexuality, and the fact that he was a Muslim. Muslims are taught that homosexuality is a sin. Ryan could have chosen one over the other, but he chose both - this brought internal conflict to his personality.

According to Health Consultancy Psychology, the fact that his victims were mostly gay, and the fact that he skewered some of them in the anus, meant that he was thinking of homosexuality during the murders.

It could also be pointed out that there was some truth in the defense's statement when they said that Ryan was insane. The fact that he took up modeling as a career meant he wanted attention, a sure sign of narcissism. Many serial killers have this trait, and judging by the way

Ryan handled his imprisonment and trials (he sang songs and wrote a book), it was clear that he wanted to attract attention.

It is, however, hard to know for sure because there was no formal release of the psychiatric examinations done upon him. Another surprising fact about this singing serial killer was his relationship with his mother. Ryan claimed that he detested his mother because she had illicit affairs during his childhood - she even reached the point of sleeping with her own daughter's husband.

Still, Ryan donated the proceeds of his book to her, and he still announced that he wanted to marry a woman in order to please her. These, according to some psychologist, were attempts to gain his mother's favor, because like everyone else, Ryan wanted acceptance from the woman who'd given birth to him.

In some stories, Ryan indicated that he picked up the gay men he killed. It was contradicting, to say the least, because why would you pick up men only to kill them when they made a move on you? A psychiatrist explained that it was his way of being in control - that he wanted to be the one to make the first move, if not, then he felt cheap.

That being said, one can only wonder what will become of The Singing Serial Killer. Will the death penalty be carried out, or will his appeal on the grounds of insanity save his life?

Chapter 6: Victim For Sale

Bobby Joe Long was born as Robert Joseph Long on October 14, 1953 in Kenova, West Virginia to parents Joe and Louella. The marriage was dysfunctional, because Joe and Louella's relationship was "sporadic," in fact, they were married twice, but they also divorced twice.

Due to this, young Bobby spent his time traveling between Southern Florida (where Louella lived) and West Virginia (where Joe stayed). Records said that Bobby slept beside his mother until he turned 13. Because he was born with an extra x chromosome (female identifying chromosome), Bobby developed breasts during his teenage years, resulting in him being severely teased by his fellow students.

Many people believed that Bobby's hatred for women started with his mother, who worked in a bar, and as result, often wore "racy" clothes - she was also reported to have brought different men home.

In his childhood (1959), Bobby suffered two violent accidents which may have affected the man he became. The first accident, when he fell down the stairs, and on the second, he was struck by a car which resulted in an irreparable jaw injury.

Starting Early

Criminal mind-wise, Bobby started early. He was accused of rape in the 1970s but was acquitted due to lack of evidence. At that time, he was already dating his wife to be, Cynthia Bartlett, and in 1974, the two got married. Soon enough, they had kids: a son and a daughter.

Becoming parents was not something they planned, so the relationship was put to the test. Then Bobby suffered another accident when a vehicle hit him while he was on his motorcycle. Hospitalized for weeks, Cynthia claimed that her husband changed after the accident: while he was really hot-tempered, he became even more so - to the point that he would become physically violent.

His sex drive also became more demanding and intense. In the 1980's, it was clear that Cynthia and Bobby should end the marriage, so Cynthia filed for a divorce, while Bobby immediately moved in with a lady friend, Sharon Richards, who, in turn, accused him of rape and battery.

In the first trial, he was found guilty, but during the

retrial, he was acquitted. The disturbing fact was, around this time, he was also found guilty of sending a sexually-infused letter and photograph to a girl in Florida, who was just 12 years old.

Bobby's punishment was a short jail sentence and a probation period. In 1984, his first planned rape would take place.

Searching the Classifieds

The reason why Bobby was known as the Classified Ads Rapist was because of his unique way of finding his victims. He looked for "For Sale" houses listed in the classified ads of the broadsheet, then he'd go there armed, and rape the female homeowner.

The first victim was the owner of a New Port Richey, Florida home. Authorities indicated that there could be more than 50 rape cases - all of the victims were found through classified ads (of for sale houses, household items, and furniture). Soon enough, the Classified Ads Rapist would turn into the Classified Ads Serial Killer.

These assaults were performed in many areas, but mostly

in Miami, Ocala, Fort Lauderdale, and Dade County. Aside from finding them through classified ads, his MO also consisted of learning if the woman was alone, if she was, then he would politely ask to use the bathroom so that he could prepare his "rape kit". After that, the brutal rape would take place.

Starting the Game

Four years after beginning his rape spree, Bobby felt that the thrill of sexually assaulting women was losing its touch - he needed to do something more. So after he raped a prostitute named Artis Wick in March of 1984, he felt discontented - the only remedy to make him satisfied was to kill her. And so he did.

On May of the same year, while driving along Nebraska Avenue in Tampa, Bobby saw Lana Long; she was obviously walking to her destination, and was in need of a ride. Bobby played the good Samaritan. He pulled over beside Lana, asked politely if she wanted a lift, and when she replied in the affirmative, they headed to the bar which was Lana's destination.

Except they never reached the bar, only a secluded area

near it. Bobby then brandished a knife at the innocent woman and threatened to kill her if she didn't do as he wished. Still having some fight left in her, Lana struggled and screamed, forcing Bobby to drive further away. When they got there, he raped the woman and strangled her to death.

It was mother's day (May 13) when Lana's body was discovered - she was lying face down, her hands tied behind her back, and her feet wide apart. Raped and strangled to death - by this time, the simple process was boring Bobby, so he became more vicious in his killing spree.

His third victim was Michelle Simms, 22 years old, a prostitute, and someone who was struggling with her drug addiction. After Bobby raped her, he bludgeoned her with a club, slashed her throat, and finally, strangled the life out of her. Although the MO in Lana's murder and that of Michelle's were noticeably different, the authorities were still able to connect the two. This was because they found a carpet fiber (red trilobal nylon) on the two bodies.

The Need for More

Experts suggest that it was Bobby's hatred for his mother that drove him to kill women - after all, if you look closely, his victims were mostly prostitutes, women he could easily connect to his mother who worked in a bar, wore skimpy clothes, and brought home short-term boyfriends.

But one should not dismiss the fact that Bobby didn't confine his assaults and killings to just prostitutes. In fact, his 4th victim, Elizabeth Loudenback was never a fast woman, and neither was she a drug user. Elizabeth just happened to be at the wrong place, at the wrong time. Her badly decomposed body was found 17 days after she was killed, in Turkey Cliff Reservoir.

Unlike the others, she was fully clothed when discovered; she also had the same red trilobal fiber found on Lana's and Michelle's body.

The fifth victim was another prostitute, Chanel Williams, whom Bobby didn't strangle (although it appeared that he had tried); instead, he took his gun and shot her in the head. After her, two more followed, Kimberly Hoops and Karen Dinsfriend, but the turning point was when Bobby took 17 year old Lisa McVey Noland.

According to police reports, Lisa was bicycling when Bobby kidnapped her and forced her to perform fellatio, after that, he brought her to his apartment, where he raped her repeatedly and showered with her. For 26 hours, Bobby treated Lisa as his personal sex slave before releasing her, alive.

It would be Lisa's statement which would bring the police to Bobby. However, he would still be able to kill two more women before the authorities finally apprehended him.

Arrest and Conviction

When Lisa gave her statement to the police, she was able to provide a good description of the car. This led them to Robert Joseph Long - he was arrested in November of 1984, and when his house was searched, they found the red carpet lining the staircase. A simple laboratory exam proved that the fiber on the victims' bodies and the fiber on his carpet, matched.

The trial ran smoothly as Bobby also admitted to many of the murders; as if he had deliberately left Lisa alive so that the police could capture him, and as if he was getting tired of the game he started and was just biding his time. This, according to some psychiatrists, was possible - some serial killers, really leave clues so that their spree will be ended.

As of now, Bobby Long is serving the following sentences: 1 five year sentence, 1 death sentence, 28 life sentences, and four 99 year sentences. He's still on death row in Florida.

Chapter 7: Impressing My Girlfriend, Svetlana

What will a man do if his girlfriend often criticizes him by telling him he is too "soft"? Most men would head to the nearest gym and build some muscles, some would read blogs on the internet and take tips on how to become the ultimate alpha male.

A few would not change anything in themselves - maybe they would just change their *girlfriend*, especially if he felt that she didn't like the real him. Alexander Bychkov from Russia was different; he opted to kill and eat 11 people, just so he could be more masculine.

Alexander Bychkov

Born in April 1, 1988, Alexander Bychkov had a difficult childhood. His mother was a drunk, and soon enough, his father, too, turned into one. Clearly, his parents were in no shape to raise a child, so it was his paternal grandmother who bought the house for the small family.

Two years after he was born, Sergei, Alexander's younger brother, was born, and after that, everything went downhill. His father took his own life, and according to neighbors, it was because of his mother's alcoholism and infidelity.

When Alexander turned 5 years old, he was forced to play the role of a little adult. His mother would make him work long hours in their vegetable garden, so that they could eat. If not that chore, the boys had to go from one neighbor's house to the next to collect metal scraps for money. Should they return without money, they would be badly beaten.

The abuse perhaps made them resort to stealing from the townspeople, and most of the time, they were caught, but because of pity (in relation to their mother's abuse), the residents would let them go without punishment.

In the late 2000s, when Alexander was in college, Sergei was involved in an accident (he was "thrown out of the car while it was in motion") which resulted in brain injuries requiring surgery. Alexander dropped out of college in order to take care of Sergei, who survived the ordeal, but was disabled.

Chill down the spine

Towards the end of 2012, the Volga Region police in Russia were almost done with their investigation into a case that would give the most cold hearted person a chill down their spine. The cannibal, Alexander Bychkov, had gutted at least 9 corpses and eaten their flesh so that his girlfriend would find him more manly. Of course it wasn't entirely her fault because she had no idea what he was doing.

The victims were drifters, or homeless people. Alexander thought that should they disappear, there wouldn't be a fuss, because no one would come looking for them. His usual manner of killing them was through butchering, using a simple kitchen knife.

The murders happened in Penza, and the half-eaten remains were buried in Belinsky, southwest of the region. The twisted thing about Alexander was how he carefully chose which body part to consume. Most of the time, he would separate the heart and the liver, so he could "enjoy" them later.

Most people wanted the case to be just a legend - something produced by rumors, but when the Police inspected the burial sites, they found the decomposing remains.

Pot Calling the Kettle Black

Aside from the practicality of choosing homeless men, police also found out that Alexander was nursing a hidden grudge against them - allegedly, he hated people who abused liquor, resorted to being beggars, and those who subjected themselves to a rough lifestyle.

According to Pravda.ru, Alexander didn't perform his crimes in haste, in fact, he prepared, physically, mentally, and emotionally. First, he would read the cases of similar serial killers. He'd take his time in studying what they did and what went wrong with their plans. Then, he would create or prepare his weapon, and finally, he would arrange things so as to hide even the smallest trace of his presence.

Still, like other serial killers, he would grow tired of his escapades and would wish to be caught.

Road to Hell

The first murder happened on September 7, 2009. Yevgeni Zhidgov was old - 60 years old was just the right age to retire and live on his pension, which he had worked hard for. On that tragic day, Yevgeni went to the city to fill out some forms to draw up his pension; perhaps after that, he planned on taking a well deserved break, sadly though, this didn't happen.

When Alexander saw him in a local tavern, he offered to let the old man stay the night at his home; finding it convenient, Yevgeni agreed. But the moment he fell asleep, the thoughtful young man turned vicious and stabbed him repeatedly until he died.

After that, most of Alexander's victims were beggars and alcoholics. Reports state that he lured his victims to his house, or other "lonely" places before he would kill them using a knife or a hammer. After that he would mutilate and dismember the bodies and bury them in his backyard, or in the landfill.

Law authorities suspected that he killed on warmer months not just so the decomposition process would be hastened, but also because migrant workers were present in the area. That meant that police would suspect migrant workers as the killer. One person (unspecified) suspected him of being the perpetrator and even tried to blackmail him, so Alexander responded by killing him, too.

The first discovered remains were that of Sergei Berezovsky, one of his mother's ex-lovers. The problem with Rambo's (he called himself that) case was the emergence of another Alexander, Alexander Zhuplov, an insane man who admitted to the murders he hadn't committed. The police found him guilty, though, and sent him to a mental institution.

On January of 2012, Alexander broke the window of a hardware store so he could steal some knives and approximately $300. He was caught, but when the police questioned him, he began telling them about the corpses which were buried behind his house.

Although the confession seemed unbelievable, the officers couldn't afford to ignore it, so they attended his home, where the truth was revealed. They found Alexander's kill book, or his diary (the author was named "lone wolf"), which contained all his crimes, in detail. The book mentioned 11 people, but even with extensive searches, the Police were only able to recover 9.

The cannibal's time was spent watching television shows and reading books, the topics pertaining to heinous crimes and serial killers. When asked why he did such atrocities, he only answered that it gave him more confidence, something that he needed because his girlfriend, Svetlana, kept on calling him "soft" and "a doormat".

Although the crime was shocking, Igor Yanushev, a psychiatrist, admitted that such cases are common in Russia, even though the country is socially advanced. He even said that cannibalism here (in Russia) is more prosaic, but the scale is more impressive, compared to the cases of other nation.

If Alexander is proven sane, he would be facing a lifetime in prison, but Dr. Igor confided that most cannibals spent their time in a medical facility rather than a penitentiary. As of now, his examination indicates that he has a mixed personality disorder, but is still competent to stand trial.

Found guilty of 9 murders (because two bodies couldn't be recovered), he is currently sentenced to life in prison. Lyubov Zhuplov, the mother of Alexander Zuphlov (the insane man who admitted to the murders), has petitioned the court to review her son's case.

Chapter 8: Killing in Retirement Years

Most serial killers share the same childhood - perhaps, he or she lacked the required parental love, or they were bullied and harassed while growing up. Some had unfortunate accidents which resulted in severe head injuries that could have caused their criminal state of mind.

Still, their killing spree would begin in their late teenage years, or may be in their middle adulthood, not usually in their retirement. Ray and Faye Copeland were different; from loving parents and grandparents, they turned into heartless killers who slayed homeless men in their residence, before using the victims' meager clothing as their own blanket.

Dead's Warmth in Winter Time

In October of 1989, the Police in Missouri received a disturbing tip: human remains were hidden in the farmland belonging to an old couple, Faye and Ray Copeland. Wishing for the best and expecting the worst, they headed out to the area to investigate, but not before doing their homework.

Police officers found out that Ray Copeland was involved in a livestock scam. When they arrived at their house, they made it seem like the visit was about the scam, but in reality, the other officers were already searching the area.

Soon enough, they found 5 shallow graves, each of which contained badly decomposing human remains. After a postmortem examination, it was revealed that the victims were shot in the head at close range. Further searches of the farmhouse yielded a registry, where farmhands who worked for the Copelands were listed; most of the laborers were transients or drifters.

Interestingly, 12 of the names in the registry were marked with "x" and in those 12, the five victims were included. A .22 caliber rifle was also discovered in the house and when it was examined, it matched the gunshot wounds of the victims. The most staggering of all the evidence was the quilt, which Faye created using the victims' clothing.

The five victims who kept them warm during winter were identified as: Dennis Murphy, Jimmie Dale Harvey, Wayne Warner, John Freeman, and Paul Jason.

Background

Ray Copeland (born on December 30, 1914) had been one of the victims of the Great Depression. Due to this, he spent his time (together with his family) moving around, struggling to get by day after day. Ray also started out young when it came to crime and fraud.

He was known to forge checks, and would often involve innocent people in livestock scams. When he was caught, he received a year in jail as his punishment. In 1940, his jail sentence ended, and once released, he met Faye Della Wilson (born in August 4, 1921). The two married quickly and had a few children together, making their financial needs tougher.

To make ends meet, Ray continued forging checks and performing his livestock scam activities, but because of his bad reputation, the family had to move around a lot. From time to time, Ray was caught and was put in jail, so he developed a new way of making illegal money without being detected.

The plan was simple and effective: because of his bad reputation, he wouldn't be able to buy cattle on his own, he needed help: he decided to hire transient laborers. Once employed, the farmhand would go to the market to buy cattle using Ray's bad checks.

After receiving the cattle, Ray would immediately sell them to have authentic money. For a while, this strategy worked, but some more scams later and he was caught. Placed in jail again, Ray decided to improve his strategy.

Instead of hiring the same farmhands, he would hire different ones each time - that way, there wouldn't be a single connection to him. Like the previous technique, this too, worked for a while, but it also lead to his capture. He hired a farmhand named Jack McCormick, and when Jack saw a couple of human remains at their home, he quickly called the Crime Stoppers Hotline.

According to reports, although the authorities were a little skeptical about the claim, they still chose to confirm it. So, with more than a dozen officers, bloodhounds, and a search warrant, they entered the house in the pretense of investigating another fraud.

In Denial and Insanity

Learning that 12 workers were marked in the registry and only finding five bodies made the authorities suspicious - there could be more corpses. The only way they could obtain the information on the other burial sites was to get it from the couple themselves, but neither of them budged.

Faye was offered an appealing bargain: provide the police with the information on the whereabouts of the 7 other bodies, and her case would be reduced from murder to conspiracy. This was a huge offer - murder was punishable by death, but conspiracy only meant less than a year in prison as a punishment. Still, Faye Copeland stood by her unbelievable statement: she knew nothing about the murders.

As for Ray, at first he wanted to plead not guilty by virtue of insanity, but later on, he appealed for a bargain - the police refused, hence their charge was still 5 counts of first degree murder. On top of that, when he learned that his wife would be killed via lethal injection, he appeared indifferent, telling the police that those things happened to some people.

Faye's lawyers stated that their client was just a victim - that she was suffering from Battered Wife Syndrome, a condition where the woman was left with little to no choice but to follow her abusive husband's wishes. The court believed that Faye was really abused, but they still thought the murders were inexcusable, hence their verdict stayed at it was - the couple were found guilty on 5 counts of first degree murder.

According to them, the fact that Faye created a quilt out of the victims' clothes meant that she knew of her husband's crime and did nothing to stop him.

Oldest Couple To Be Sentenced To Death

Although the two were the oldest couple to be placed on death row, neither of them died through execution: Ray died in 1993, and Faye's verdict was commuted into a life sentence. In 2002, Faye was released due to her declining condition and a year after that, she died in a nursing home at the age of 83.

Chapter 9: Railway Station of Death

Born on October 25, 1879, Fritz Haarmann was known as the Butcher or the Vampire of Hanover, Germany. From 1918 to 1924, Fritz sexually assaulted, murdered, mutilated, and dismembered at least 24 people - all of whom were young boys or young men.

Vicious

From police reports, the victims ages ranged from 10 to 22 years old and all of them would be lured into one of the three addresses which Fritz used over the period of his killing spree. Victims would often believe him because he appeared harmless, in fact, most of the time, he was the bearer of good news, promising the young boy a job, or cheap accommodation. If that didn't work, sometimes Fritz pretended to arrest them just so they would follow him.

Once inside the apartment, the victim would be well provided for: he'd be offered food, drinks, and relaxation, until his guard was down. At that moment, Fritz would then give him a "love bite". Love bite was the term Fritz used to describe how he would bite *hard* on the victim's Adam's apple (or trachea) while he was strangling the life out of the youth. This would result in air hunger, and ultimately, death.

After the gruesome murder, Fritz would dismember the body before disposing of the body parts usually into the Leine River. However, his first and last victim were disposed of with less violence. The first one was simply buried while the last one was thrown into the river - there was no mutilation or dismemberment.

Fritz's viciousness didn't end there: the possessions of the victims would still be used. Some were stolen so that Fritz and his lover, Hans Grans, could use them, if that wasn't possible, then they would sell the valuables on the black market through contacts they had obtained over the years. The worst scenario was when the victims' possessions were used as gifts to Hans' and/or Fritz' acquaintances.

It is believed although never proven that he also sold their meat and flesh on the black market; with the right connection, he could simply declare the flesh as horse meat or pork. Many followers of the case believed he did do this and police reports confirmed that Fritz had been selling contraband meat that was boneless, diced, or minced. I

f someone asked him where he obtained the meat, he only responded by saying it came from "Karl", but the stories varied depending on who asked.

The first confirmed victim was a young man named Friedel Rothe, 17 years old. On September 27, 1918, Friedel was last seen by his friends in Fritz' apartment, so when he didn't return, they told the police what they knew.

Pressured by Friedel's family, they searched Fritz' home, but they didn't find the 17 year old boy. Later, however, during the investigation, Fritz admitted that had the police only looked further, they would have found Friedel's severed head behind his stove.

Birth of an Accomplice

Hans Grans was at his wits' end: on October 1, 1919, he and his father had a huge fight, so he left even though he had nowhere else to go. The only place available was the Hanover station, and even there, he had to sell his old clothes for food. After two weeks of mindless meandering and having no direction, he met Fritz Haarmann, whom people from the station labeled as homosexual.

With no choice, Grans decided to sell his body; he was a straight guy, but when you need money to survive, you have to be creative. So, he initiated the contact with Fritz, and he didn't fail. Even in Fritz' side of the story, he said that Hans was like a son to him, and that he "pulled him from the ditch" and made sure that the "dogs wouldn't get him".

It turned out though, that Hans just used Fritz as a meal ticket and the latter accepted it. According to Fritz, Hans usually mocked him with "threats and accusations against him" and during some heated arguments, the younger of the two lovers would often leave.

After a while though, Fritz would go to Hans and beg him to come back despite the fact that he knew he was only being used. The Vampire's exact words were: "I had to have someone I meant everything to."

Still, it was a mutual understanding; Fritz got the companionship and affection he yearned for and Hans helped him in his murders.

Two is better than one

The next murders performed by Fritz were mostly centered on young men (often commuters, runaways, and prostitutes) whom he met at the Hanover railway station. The second murder happened on February 12 1923, when he met a 17 year old pianist, Fritz Franke at the Hanover Railway station.

The young man was invited into Fritz's apartment at Neue Straße where he was introduced to Hans and two female acquaintances (one of whom was said to be Hans' female lover). Later, during the investigation, Hans' female lover confided that during that night, Hans whispered in her ear and said: "He's going to be trampled on today…"

When the two women left the apartment, pianist Fritz was apparently still alive, but when they returned the next day, he was already gone: The Butcher of Hanover said that he had travelled to Hamburg. Albeit Hans' previous comment to his female lover was a little suspicious, it was unclear if he knew of the murder.

Fritz himself reported to the authorities that after the murder, Hans arrived at the apartment unannounced and when he saw the victim's nude body on the bed, he simply asked, "When shall I come back?" More than one month after Fritz Franke was murdered, Fritz The Vampire encountered another would-be victim.

Wilhelm Schulze was on the way to work when he encountered Fritz Haarmann, and since then, he was never seen again. Unlike other victims though, Wilhelm's was hard to confirm because no remains were discovered, but his clothing was found in the possession of Elisabeth Engel, Fritz' landlady, at the time of his arrest.

After 17 year old Wilhelm, two more victims were killed in the Neue Straße apartment: 19 year old Hans Sonnenfeld, who went missing on May 31 and never returned (Fritz was seen wearing his distinctive yellow overcoat after the murder), and 16 year old Roland Huch, who disappeared on May 23 after telling a friend that he was running away from home to join the marines. After these two murders, Fritz left the Neue Straße apartment and moved to 2 Rote Reihe.

Terrors at 2 Rote Reihe

On June 9, 1923, Fritz moved to a single room attic

apartment at 2 Rote Reihe, and within just two weeks, he found another prey to slay. Fritz didn't look far; his next victim was the thirteen year old son of his neighbor. On June 25, 1923, Ernst Ehrenberg went out to run an errand for his father, but like so many others who had encountered the Vampire of Hanover, he never returned.

Post arrest, his cap and suspenders were recovered in Fritz's apartment. One month after Ernst disappeared, the 18 year old office clerk Heinrich Struß also went missing. The disappearance was reported by his aunt whom he lived with.

A month after Heinrich was murdered, Paul Bronichewsky, who was on his way to Bochum city, was also killed. Reports said Paul spent the entire summer working with his uncle in Sachsen-Anhalt. Police suspect that he must have got off a train in the Hanover station and encountered Fritz. Similar to Ernst's case, many of Heinrich and Paul's belongings were also recovered in Fritz' apartment post arrest.

On September 30, 1923, Richard Gräf, who was only 17 years old, told his family that he met someone from the Hanover station who could give him a good job. After that, he never returned.

On October 12, 1923, Wilhelm Erdner failed to come back home, and when his parents reported him missing, they told the police that prior his disappearance, he had become close to a certain Detective Fritz Honnerbrock (one of Fritz' Haarmann's aliases). On October 20, Hans and Fritz sold Wilhelm's bicycle.

Within seven days of selling the property of their latest victim, Fritz killed again - twice. His victims were 15 year old and 13 year old and both of them were last seen at the Hanover railway station.

On November 10, 1923, 17 year old carpenter-to-be Adolf Hannappel went missing in the railway station. Witnesses attested that they had seen Fritz and Hans there while pointing at Adolf - a few minutes later and the trio left together. It was the last known sighting of Adolf. Less than a month after that, on December 6, Adolf Hennies disappeared.

During the investigation, Fritz would admit to dismembering the body, but he denied any hand in his murder. According to him, he simply saw the body lying on the bed - without his "love bite" - together with Hans and another accomplice, Hugo Wittkowski.

When Hans heard this statement, he vehemently disputed it. Due to their contradicting statements and the fact that there was no evidence, neither Fritz nor Hans was convicted for Adolf Hennies murder.

Evidence

In 1924, Fritz Haarmann, the Vampire of Hanover killed 13 more people - the youngest was 10 year old Freidrich Abeling. There were instances when Fritz himself couldn't remember the murder because of how random and how often he did it; the only clue would be the discovery of the victims' possessions in his apartment.

In May of 1924, 2 children innocently playing near the Leine River saw a human skull. When the police reached the scene, they identified the victim as someone who was between the ages of 18 to 20. Their main concern was determining whether the murdered happened in the river or if the skull was only thrown in the area.

What was worse, they believed it to be an isolated case. However, when a second skull was recovered near the area, and he too was aged between 18 to 20 years old, the police began suspecting a serial killer was at large. This was supported when another set of playing children discovered a sack, which was filled with human bones.

On June 8, hundreds of concerned citizens joined the search efforts. They combed the area surrounding the Leine River, and when they found more human bone fragments, the police decided to drag the river. And when they did, 500 more human bone fragments were found.

Lab reports showed that the victims had been stabbed, and all of them belonged to 22 different people - all male and young in age. Examinations also determined that half of the remains had been there for quite some time, while the other half were newly transferred.

Because he was a known homosexual and he had previously been suspected in the disappearance of Friedel Rothe, the police quickly placed Fritz Haarmann under surveillance, which started on June 18. On the night of June 24, Fritz and a young man named Karl Fromn (15) were seen fighting.

When the police approached, Fritz insisted that they should arrest Karl immediately because he was forging documents. The authorities played along for a while, but after arresting Karl, they interviewed him, and that's when they knew that Fritz Haarmann could be the serial killer in Hanover. Allegedly, Karl had been living with Fritz for the past 4 days and in that period, the man had repeatedly raped him, sometimes at knife point.

From there the investigation moved forward: they ransacked Fritz' apartments and found many belongings of the victims, more over, witnesses (mostly neighbors) attested that many teenagers had come and gone from his living quarters. Worse, the Butcher of Hanover was often seen leaving his home with a large sack or bag, which according to one witness who followed him discreetly, he disposed of in the Leine River.

When all the evidence started to mount up, the verdict was swift: execution. The vampire of Hanover was sentenced to death and was executed on April 15, 1925; he was beheaded by guillotine. Before his death, Fritz left a letter to Hans' father, telling everyone that Hans was innocent.

As a result a retrial was ordered, and instead of murder, Hans was charged with aiding and abetting with two murders to which he was punished with 2 concurrent 12 year sentences. After serving his sentence, he continued to live in Hanover until he died in 1975.

Why he did it?

Growing up, Fritz was naturally effeminate even though he had the build of a strong man. He viewed his father as a rival and it lasted until the day he died. Barring the unhealthy childhood (stern father, overbearing mother, and later on, poverty), laboratory reports also indicate that Fritz' brain had a trace of meningitis.

Chapter 10: Unstoppable Randall

The I-5 Killer or I-5 Bandit, these were the names Randall Woodfield was called because of his notorious slayings, assaults, and robberies on the Interstate 5 which runs through Washington, Oregon, and California. Although he was only known for three murders, police suspected him to be responsible for as many as 44 killings.

Simply Him

Unlike most serial killers, Randall (born on December 26, 1950 in Oregon) never came from an impoverished family - his parents were of the middle class. The entire Woodfield household wasn't dysfunctional; there was no report of abuse or neglect, and he was cared and provided for.

Randall flourished under his parents' care. He was involved in sports and was even the star player at Newport High School and at Portland State University football team. There was nothing wrong with Randall's family, but there was something wrong with him.

In his adolescence, Randall seemed to love sexual

exhibitionism. His first arrest happened during his high school years, but because the coach didn't want him to be kicked out of the football team, he did everything to conceal the case.

Unfortunately, even though Randall was a great player, his mental problem with exhibitionism wasn't attended to, so it only worsened. In the 1970s, his public indecency reached its peak, that even though he was already included in the 1974 NFL draft, he was still kicked out of the roster.

Escalating Quickly

In 1975, some women in Portland reported that they had been assaulted by a knife-wielding man; said man would force them to perform oral sex before he robbed their hand bags. Due to this, the police assigned some female officers in disguise as random women, and during their operation, they caught Randall Woodfield - with marked money in his hands.

He was sentenced to spend 10 years in prison for second-degree robbery, but because of parole, he only spent 4 - he was freed in July of 1979. From the moment he was released, something evil in Randall might have been unleashed, for now he not only wanted to assault women - he desired to kill them. And kill he did.

Cherie Ayers was Randall's high school classmate; on October 9, 1980, she was found dead in Portland, Oregon. Her head had been bludgeoned and she had multiple stab wounds to the neck. Law authorities suspected and questioned Randall, but he declined any polygraph tests.

His answers, according to the officers, were evasive and deceptive, but because his blood type didn't match the semen found in the crime scene, he wasn't convicted. A month later, Darci Fix and Doug Altic were murdered in the latter's Portland apartment and a gun was found to be missing from the residence. Although Darci was a former lover of one of Randall's closest friends, the police didn't immediately draw any connection.

A String of Crimes

On December 9, 1980, a man wearing a false beard robbed a gas station in Vancouver, Washington. 4 days later, a man bearing the same description, held up an ice cream parlor. The day after that, the same man accosted a drive-in restaurant in Albany, and one week later, in Seattle, the fake-beard wearing man sexually assaulted a waitress in a chicken restaurant.

According to her, the man locked her up in the restroom, forced her to masturbate him, and then left her terrified. The man was armed. Before the burglar and offender left Seattle, he was still able to rob another ice cream parlor.

At this point, the police had already named him the I-5 Bandit, because of his penchant for committing the crimes along the corridors of Interstate 5. The string of crimes continued, to the point that he robbed the same place twice. Once he also forced a female cashier to expose her breasts for him, and in another case, he shot a grocery store worker.

In January 14, Randall, while still wearing his false beard, broke into and entered a small apartment where two sisters lived; one was only 8 years old and the other was 10. Despite their young age, Randall still sexually assaulted them. He then entered an office in Salem and raped two women; Shari Hull (who was killed) and Beth Wilmot (who was left wounded).

The next month, on February 3, 1981, a mother and child

were killed in their home at mountain Gate, California. Their bodies were found side by side in their bed. Postmortem examinations showed that the child had been sodomized before the murder. The next day, two more women were kidnapped and raped, one was from Yreka, and the other was from Ashland, Oregon.

From here, the crimes went on and on, as if Randall was unstoppable. In fact, in February 28, although the police had centered their investigation on Randall, he was still able to perform three more sexual assaults and robbery.

Arrest And Conviction

On March 3, 1981, Salem Police Department brought Randall in for questioning, and after two days, they had a warrant to search his apartment. According to the authorities, they were looking for someone who was familiar with the areas near Interstate 5, and someone who had the props for the false beard.

Additionally, most of the sexual assault victims reported they had been tied up with tape. Although it wasn't mentioned if the false beard was recovered, the tape found in his apartment matched those used on the victims.

Considering the amount of crimes Randall had committed (robbery, sexual assault, sodomy, murders, battery, etc.) Randall's punishment was a lifetime in prison (for Shari's murder) plus 165 years for his other offenses. As of now, he is still in Oregon State Penitentiary. Many people (even the police) believed that Randall was connected to at least 44 murders, however they can't be proven.

Conclusion

Thank you again for purchasing this book!

We have discussed 10 cases of serial killers in this book; we've gotten a glimpse of their childhood years, of their previous ambitions, and of their desires. All of them, except for the Doodler, were apprehended, and some were even sentenced to death.

In your own opinion, were the killers featured in this book insane? Or were they just pure evil? While it's true that many of them suffered from unhealthy formative years, some were raised normally, so what was the determining factor?

Perhaps, the reason could be trivial because the most important thing is for them to be caught, but knowing what made them the monsters we've known them to be, will surely help in profiling future criminals.

If you enjoyed this book, do you think you could leave me a review on Amazon? Just search for this title and my name on Amazon to find it. Thank you so much, it is very much appreciated!

Check Out My Other Books

Below you'll find some of my other popular books that are popular on Amazon and Kindle as well. You can visit my author page on Amazon to see other work done by me. (Brody Clayton).

True Murder Stories
Women Who Kill
Serial Killers
Cold Cases True Crime
Serial Killers – Volume 2
Cold Cases True Crime – Volume 2
True Crime
True Crime – Volume 2
True Crime – Volume 3
Serial Killers True Crime
Serial Killers True Crime – Volume 2
Serial Killers True Crime – Volume 3

Serial Killers True Crime – Volume 4

You can simply search for these titles on the Amazon website with my name to find them.

Serial Killers True Crime
LIBRARY BUGS BOOKS

Like FREE books?

Would you like them delivered to you every week?

Do you like non-fiction books on a huge range of different topics?

We send out FREE e-books every week so we can share our books with the world!

We have FREE books every week on AMAZON that we send to our email list. If you want in, then visit the link below to sign up and sit back and wait for new books to be sent straight to your inbox!

It couldn't be simpler!

www.LibraryBugs.com

If you want FREE books delivered straight to your inbox, then visit the link above and soon you'll be receiving a great list of FREE e-books every week!

Enjoy :)

Printed by Amazon Italia Logistica S.r.l.
Torrazza Piemonte (TO), Italy